Faith Needs a Miracle

By

Joan E. Murray

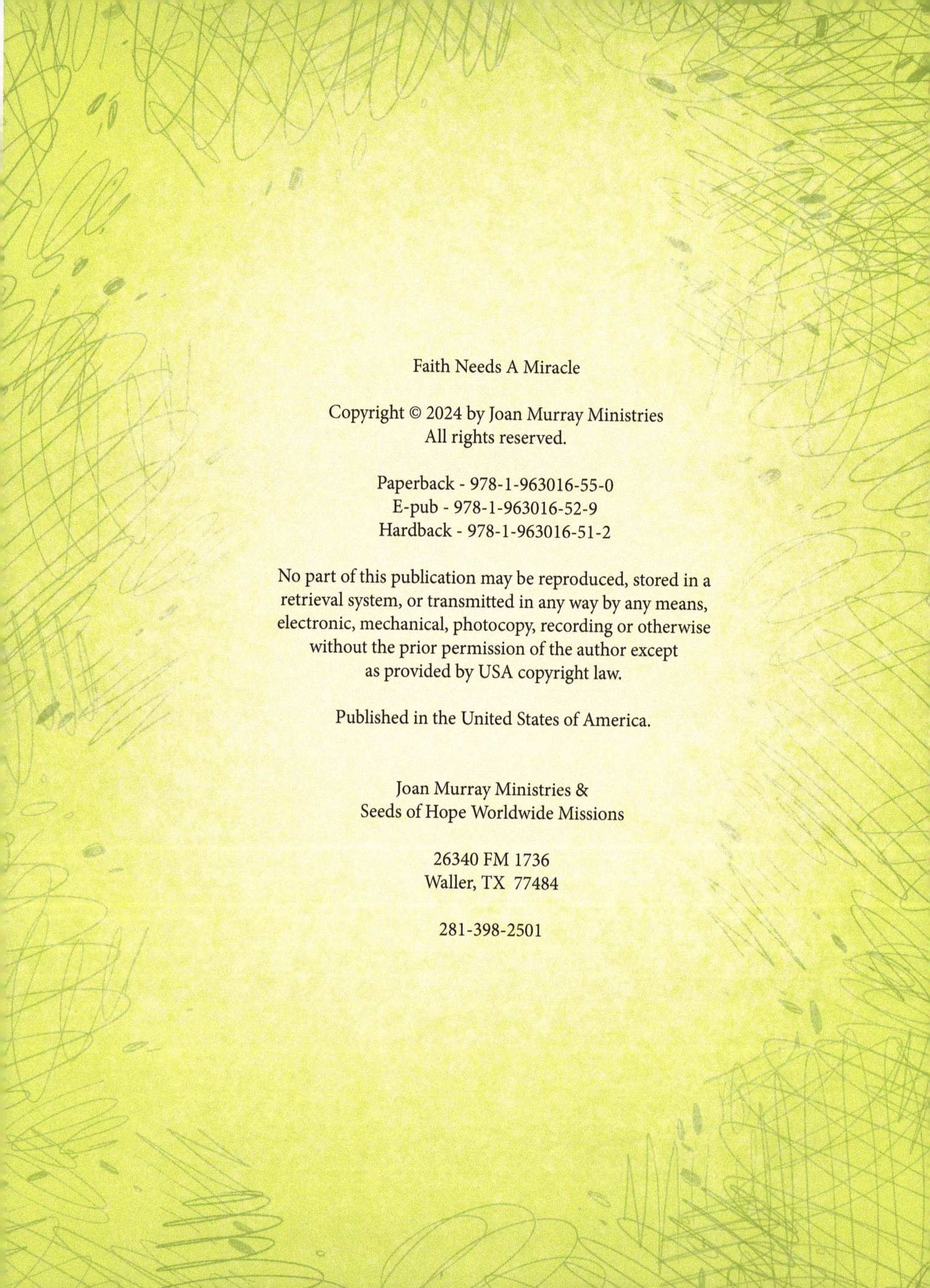

Dedicated to sick children
and their families.
Healing belongs
to all children.

"Daughter, what's wrong?" There was no response.
Going over to Faith, Ada asked again. "Faith, what's wrong?"
Ada's voice trembled with concern for her daughter.
She looked into Faith's beautiful brown eyes. Faith looked
blankly at her while holding her head and screaming.
 "Mommy, Mommy," Faith cried, her voice filled with pain,
"Please, I can't bear it anymore, "help me!"

Ada didn't know what to do
because her daughter wasn't
physically hurt.
Faith couldn't tell her what
was hurting because she
didn't know.

Watching closely over Faith for a few days without seeing any changes and things worsening, Ada prayed.
"God, help me."
Listening intently, Ada heard a soft whisper. "Go find Jesus."
Sighing with deep relief, Ada felt a surge of hope as she knew what to do.

Leaving Faith in the care of a trusted family member, Ada, with unwavering determination, hurried to find Jesus.

As Ada moved through the bustling crowd, her heart
pounding in her chest, she asked everyone she met,
"Where is Jesus? I need His help right now."
"I need His help right now," Ada shouted.
The people ignored her, so she shouted louder,
"Please tell me, where is Jesus?"
Ada approached a group of men and said,
"Are you Jesus' disciples?"

The men, who had been following Jesus closely, looked at each other, and one nodded.

"I need to talk to Jesus," Ada said.

One replied, "He's taking a break and can't be disturbed now."

"But I need to talk to Him," Ada exclaimed.

Ignoring the men, she kept searching for Jesus. "I must find Him. My daughter is sick and needs His help!" Ada knew Jesus was the only one who could give her a miracle.

Seeing another group of men talking quietly, Ada took a deep breath and approached them.
Looking frantically around them, she spotted Jesus heading into a house.
Before anyone could stop her, she ran toward Jesus, shouting, "Jesus, Jesus!"

Jesus stopped and turned around after hearing Ada's desperate call.
Out of breath and with tears streaming down her face, Ada cried. "Jesus, have mercy on me. I need your help!" Her voice was filled with desperation.

Jesus, have mercy on me,
Ada begged, looking at
Jesus.
My daughter is sick and
needs a miracle...
Ada paused, "Jesus?"
She waited...
"Only you can
help her," she said
sorrowfully.

Jesus looked at her but didn't answer her.
"Send her away, Jesus," the disciples said, their voices filled with impatience. "She keeps making a lot of noise and bothering us."
Ada ignored them and kept looking at Jesus.

"I'm only sent to help these children," Jesus told her.
"I understand, but I still need your help," Ada replied.
"My daughter is sick, and I can't bear to see her in such pain."
Kneeling at His feet, Ada said, "Jesus, please help me."

Ada, "It's not right to take the bread from these children and feed it to someone else."

"You're right, Jesus, but... Ada trailed off, looking down.

Tilting her head to the side, Ada tapped her chin with her finger as Jesus waited for her to respond.

"You know what, Jesus?" "What, Ada?" Jesus answered?
"Even the dogs eat the bread crumbs that fall from the family's
table," Ada replied, her voice filled with unwavering faith.
"Awwwh!" Jesus said with a beaming smile.

"Ada, you have great faith," Jesus exclaimed!
Ada knew she had scored a point when she saw the smile on His face.
Jesus was pleased with my answer, Ada thought with relief.
Ada grinned. I have given Jesus the answer He needs to grant my miracle.
Yep! Ada thought, my dogs always hang around my table waiting for the crumbs to fall.
So glad I have dogs, Ada nodded, feeling relieved.

"Ada, your request is granted," said Jesus.
Trying to control her excitement, Ada grinned from cheek to cheek.
Leaving the stunned disciples staring at Jesus, Ada did a little jig and hurried home.

Rushing into her house, Ada heard loud laughter and
people talking over each other.
The atmosphere was filled with joy as she rushed in,
anxious to see her daughter, Faith.
Faith, seeing her mother, ran into her arms.

"Faith," Ada said, releasing a deep breath and looking into her
daughter's beautiful brown eyes, "you are healed!"
Ada was awed at the beautiful miracle Jesus had given her daughter.

Overwhelmed with gratitude,
Ada whispered a silent prayer.
"Thank you, Jesus. My daughter,
Faith, is free. You have given us a
wonderful miracle."

Ada watched as Faith ran into the yard to play with her cousins. Looking at her, you couldn't see the evidence of the sickness she'd been through, Ada thought.

Releasing a deep breath of thanks, Ada left Faith playing with her cousins and went to prepare a celebration meal.

The house was filled with laughter and chatter as family and friends gathered to rejoice in the miracle given to Faith.

Listen, listen, Ada said to the family and friends gathered for the celebration.
Today... I met Jesus.

He heard my desperate plea and gave Faith a miracle.
The guests listened with awe as she told of the gentleness of Jesus, His compassion and understanding. They were captivated by her words, their hearts filled with hope and faith.

Looking closely at her guests, Ada whispered again, "Jesus heard my desperate plea and gave Faith a miracle. I am so thankful Jesus changed our lives, strengthening my faith and showing me His great mercy and love."

About the Author

Joan Murray is totally committed to helping people discover their destinies. She is the founder and CEO of Joan Murray Ministries and Seeds of Hope Worldwide Missions. Joan is dedicated to teaching, training, equipping and helping people who are in various life struggles. Joan is a minister, bible teacher, author, and missionary. She has traveled extensively throughout the United States and internationally, sharing the gospel and serving the needs of the oppressed. Joan currently resides in Houston, Texas.

If you would like to know more about Joan Murray Ministries or Seeds of Hope Worldwide Missions, please get in touch with us at:
Joan Murray
Ministries & Seeds Of Hope Worldwide Missions
26340 FM 1736
Waller, TX 77848
281-398-2504
email:jmmcontactus@gmail.com
website:joanmurrayministries.org
website: www.jemmuniquegifts.com

Changing Lives Through the Power
and Truth of God's Word.

www.ingramcontent.com/pod-product-compliance
Lightning Source LLC
Chambersburg PA
CBHW041529120626
46551CB00018B/2627